Contents

P9-CLS-409

DEDICATION

This book is dedicated to my mother, Sheri Gould.
Thank you for exemplifying everything in this book.
I love you

Preface

I wrote this book because I want people to understand joy. I also want people to taste what it's like to live courageously. I want them to tap into the side of themselves that is actually unstoppable and brave. I want people to understand what personal freedom is and how it feels to chase relentlessly after true fulfillment. I want people to be successful, joyful, giving and selfless. But that doesn't happen by chance.

I believe that developing ourselves through selfless awareness of our God-given purpose is the divine design for achieving our best life. I am passionate about correcting certain illusions that run rampant in today's Self-Help world because I believe they are doing people more harm than good. I believe that you, a person trying to advance yourself, deserve to know the most efficient and truthful way to find what you seek. You deserve to understand the best way to do things– the way that will truly equip you for progress, not just claim to. This book is unique to the Motivational category because I don't simply tell you what to do or how to feel; instead, I take the time to explain the "why" behind everything I state so you can understand. That approach makes this book as philosophical as it is practical, which is an unusual mix.

This book may not be long but it is packed full of "meat." That's because I don't believe what you, my precious reader, need is another shallow, motivational mantra to repeat everyday. I believe you need real substance because you face real problems. You experience real pain, so you need real guidance, which can only come from truth. This book is the process of Selfless Development that I hope and pray each person begins to use to transform their lives; to begin experiencing a joy that doesn't shatter with pain and a fearlessness that doesn't only exist with ease. It is only by following the original design of truth and order that you can arrive at such a wondrous destination.

Love you,
Kristin Sheffer

Foreword

My name is Dr. Diana Corzo and I am a licensed Christian psychologist based in Southern California. For more than 3 decades, I've worked with patients with mild and serious mental illnesses that greatly affect their quality of life and functioning. My patients have had many issues to work through requiring delicate exploration of their thinking and trusting processes in order to experience healing and hope again. When I heard the news that Kristin was releasing a book about the process of "Selfless Development" I was intrigued and honored to be given the opportunity to endorse her and her work.

I met Kristin about 8 years ago when she was in the early stages of her rise to corporate success. Upon our initial meeting in person, my immediate impression of her was that of an intensely passionate young lady, who was driven and focused. She was both a lady *and* a tiger. I could see why others might experience her as intimidating and forceful, but I appreciated and even enjoyed her vigor! I also sensed an internal struggle going on despite her charismatic personality. We continued to develop a relationship primarily via email, by discussing topics we both felt passionately about. I anticipated the day she would focus all of that intensity and energy towards the process of growth, becoming all she was created to be.

I am happy to say that day has arrived.

Although our relationship was never clinical in nature, I had the opportunity to walk through some rough moments with her, witnessing her 'raw' and struggling self. To see her translate and shape what she has learned into a roadmap for others is an exciting milestone. Selfless Development is the product and reflection of her own journey of personal discovery explained in a way that inspires the reader to seek a similar discovery and growth process. Although young, she has acquired wisdom well beyond her years.

Selfless Development will appeal primarily to folks in their 20's and 30's because that's the time in life when you are trying to figure out who you are, what you want to do with your life, what it all means, and hopefully pursue those answers. I am excited to see a book that can benefit the 'nonpatient' who is experiencing the less extreme versions of meaninglessness or hopelessness, but is still seeking answers. I believe that when you stop growing there is no 'life' left in you and that leads to despair. *Selfless Development* is an inspirational book designed to reignite a growth process that may have stopped, stalled out, or slowed down. The principles explained in the coming pages will give you the understanding and the tools to set sail for new adventures in life, savoring each step. As both a book and a method of personal growth, selfless development is the 'right' kind of hard work. By following this type of development you will experience results, trust me. Your purpose and passion are waiting to be discovered. All you need to be is honest with yourself and willing to start examining issues from a new perspective, "the Purpose Perspective!"

Watching Kristin live out the process, allowing God to transform her life, has been a captivating experience for me as an observer. My hope is that you, her reader, will allow yourself to be ignited and inspired by this growth process as well and discover your own.

Lastly, because this book contains several abstract concepts along with many practical application tools, I recommend reading one chapter at a time. There is much to contemplate in just a few pages... If you rush you may miss certain critical issues. Journal, take a few notes and/or discuss with a trusted friend. That way, you will surely get the maximum benefit. Although she designed it to be relatively simple, the process of discovering all you were created to be is only attainable from a place of dedicated commitment to growth. As long as you enter the process with a willingness to be honest and to learn, I assure you, you will be blessed.

Prepare to be amazed because the ride to joy is both wild and crazy!

Diana M. Corzo, Psy.D
clinical psychologist

Introduction

'Short and simple' are three words that describe this book. If that's your cup of tea, then you have found a real gem. Maybe the title intrigued you, or maybe it was the cover. Whatever it is, something inside you is interested in the content of this book and I'm willing to bet it's because you identify with one of these people:

1. You feel generally content with how your life is going. You've got a steady job, a stable relationship, and maybe a few kids. You feel good and have no real complaints. You're happy but sometimes wish you could do more, be more, give more but there's just never enough time.
2. Most days you wake up feeling like the human embodiment of the word "blah." You feel a constant pressure to *"have it all together"* by now, but you don't. You wish you did but some things just didn't work out as you planned. You're frustrated, confused, and directionless. You wonder whether things would turn around if you were more disciplined. Yet, every time you set a goal, it's just a matter of time before you give up.

3. You wake up most days feeling as if there's a 20 lb. weight on your chest. The pain you feel is becoming too much to handle. The questions, fears, anger, shame and sadness seem like the only colors in your world. Your thoughts no longer help you; they haunt you. It's becoming more and more difficult to follow through on a task. You look in the mirror, realizing the person staring back at you is a stranger– a person you don't even like. Your life seems to be heading in a downward spiral, and you're just along for the ride. You honestly can't remember the last time you felt happy.

No matter where in that spectrum you fall– this book is for you. It walks you through the process that we were designed to follow in order to find true personal freedom. It begins with a crucial shift in your perspective that will change the way you view your self and your life as a whole. Then I show you how that perspective impacts your daily life.   If you want a joyful and peaceful life, it begins with taking responsibility for yourself. This puts control back into your hands! A control that enlightens you to the endless potential that you have, right there at your fingertips. If you feel any sort of discontentment, it could be because somewhere along the way, you've given up that power. You didn't mean to, but you did. Now your life is manifesting symptoms like unhappiness, frustration, apathy, depression, confusion, "feeling stuck", etc. All indicating that balance has been disturbed. To you I would say: at the core, you are so much stronger than you realize. This book will remind you of the powerhouse you really are.

In this book you can expect to receive two things:

1. The Purpose Perspective. This is the perspective that must wash over your mind in order to view yourself and your life the way it was originally intended. This perspective will break through any illusions that may be keeping your life stagnant by exposing the lies you may be believing without even realizing it. When applied, the blinders of fear and insecurity fade away leaving you exposed to the core freedom you possess through the power of choice. Just as joy is the result of our daily choices, so is unhappiness. Dependent upon our daily actions, we will either reap one or the other. Yet unhappy people usually share the belief that they are unable to affect the reason(s) for their unhappiness. They often believe they must acquire *something else* in order to be happy and end up continually frustrated by the lack thereof. The Purpose Perspective corrects that misguided thinking with the truth. You can and will create your own future!

2. My Freedom Formula. This is a three step process to begin prioritizing The Purpose Perspective as the most influential factor in your conscious thinking. Then, I give you three essential skills to begin applying this development process into your daily life. These skills, when applied, allow you to start accomplishing what you actually want to do – what you were BORN to do! Giving you a taste of real personal freedom. It is simple, but it is not easy.

As a Personal Development Coach, I watch people struggle because they believe things are more complicated than they really are. This belief quickly turns into excuses. These excuses then become justification for inaction, leading ultimately to frustration, dissatisfaction and unhappiness.

If you are not looking for a life that is overflowing with passion, kindness, strength and purpose then – *spoiler alert!* – this book may not be for you. I am going to give you a dose of tough love that may leave you uncomfortable at first. But if you are truly ready to take your life to the next level, you will see the wisdom behind my approach. The principles, truths, and perspectives I am going to share with you will absolutely change your life if you understand them.

Imagine, for a moment, a big orange wall, extending as far as you can see in both directions. In front of this wall is a person repeatedly banging their fists against it growing more and more frustrated. You approach this person and ask, "Why are you banging on this wall? Do you think it's going to move?"

Bewildered, they stare back at you and say, "Wall!? What wall? This isn't a wall. It's a door!" Stepping back to take what appears to be a second glance they begin muttering, "I guess it doesn't look like one, and it doesn't feel like one. But I know it's a door. It has to be! It has to open because it's a door. It has to open..."

I understand that poor misguided 'wall banger'. You see, for many years, that individual was me. I was controlled by fear that created many illusions within my mind. Ones that wouldn't allow me to see things as they really were. Instead, I blindly believed things were as I *wanted* them to be. I gave my all to a career I wasn't passionate about. I made money that I didn't use well. I worked very hard for someone else and was actually very content doing so. I married someone I wouldn't spend the rest of my life with. I fell for men I thought I loved when really it was desperation. I had no idea I may have a specific purpose for my life in which I was not fulfilling. ***I had no idea I was living a life of contentment but sacrificing a life of fulfillment.*** That's how blocked my mind was from understanding the importance of purpose and living life out of the mentality of gratitude. Instead, I lived out of comfort and what I perceived to be security. I wasted time, money, energy, and emotion on protecting the illusions that I so desperately clung to, because without them I was lost. At best they left me content and stagnant, but at worst they left me hopeless and angry. I was so preoccupied with turning 'walls into doors' that I stole the opportunity from myself of actually finding the door that I desperately searched for. **The concept of creating mental illusions is what I speak at length about in the coming chapters.**

At the age of 23, my life fell apart before my eyes. I experienced levels of personal failure in ways I never would have anticipated. Choices that were made by myself and the ones I loved left my life shattered into a million tiny pieces. After losing everything I thought defined my identity, I finally lost grip of who I thought I was. At core levels, I had no sense of self dignity, self confidence, self esteem, or self perception anymore. It was all lost into the abyss. I was taught from an early age the importance of taking full responsibility for my actions, which made recovering from personal failure very difficult. I felt the weight of my mistakes so entirely that it became too much to bare. The only way I could make it through each day without jumping off my 12-story balcony was by simply going numb. You see, I thought that because certain choices had been made, their consequences were imminent. (For example, because I went through a divorce at such a young age, I felt as though I was "damaged goods." I figured I'd be judged by most men who dated me after that. I felt I had to look for other divorced men, or men who had been through what I had gone through and wouldn't see me any differently.) This belief rendered me powerless over the outcome of my life from the point of failure forward because I had given up control out of guilt, pain and shame. I was simply waiting for the next consequence to take form as if I was watching a show, no idea what might come next. I took all my power and gave it to my failure.

During that time, I became exposed to a different side of life than I had known before. I actually experienced despair. Not just disappointment or fear or angst, but despair. I mean, what else do you feel when you are powerless over your life? I was used to being in control and yet I wasn't anymore. I tried to find control, peace, some semblance of sanity but everywhere I looked was useless. I was used to accessing an internal power source that allowed me to direct my future by the choices I made, and yet nothing turned out as I expected. I faced the realization that you can amass everything you're "supposed to" and still be victim to emptiness. I had money in the bank and a thriving career, but I was alone and miserable because my mind had become my worst enemy. You see, at some point, I had begun believing the lie that I was a victim. Albeit to my own worst choices, the state remained: victim. I had forgotten, or perhaps never knew to begin with, that each day presented the opportunity to direct my future.

Since the purpose of this book is not to detail my own personal story, I am not going to go into much more detail about this specific time period other than the fact that it exposed me to a dark side of life that I never want to revisit.

It was only when I became weary of waking up each day as a dead woman that I finally chose to do something about it. **I told all of my past failures, frustrations, anger, hurt, pain, guilt, shame, and confusion to go to hell. I decided that I had suffered enough and accepted that I was born for more than medicated misery.** From that point forward, I went through a process of realizing that yes, *my choices had consequences, but the way I responded to those consequences actually defined whether the choices were a failure or a success.*

(You may need to read that one last sentence again... it is extremely important.)

My road to finding personal freedom consisted primarily of being set free from my despair and anxiety. This freedom created a deep sense of gratitude that permeated every area of my life. I began to value my purpose and learned to find solace within its strength. I returned to my former reality where my daily choices actually mattered. My pivotal point came when I realized that my life was indeed in Gods hands, as He is sovereign over all. But He gives us a level of control, entrusting us to use it according to His will. This helped me realize that since I had gotten myself where I was, I should be able to get myself out. By the grace of God that is exactly what happened.

This book will explain the process I went through that took my life from toxic cycles of despair and depression to complete freedom and joy. Redefining my failure was the best decision I ever made. By allowing the grace of God to turn my pile of burnt ash into a beautiful monument of redemption, grace and strength I was able to find my freedom. Seeing that this was possible removed any hesitation I may have had to expose some tough truths to those suffering around me. Some of which don't even realize that they are suffering. The cost of a life spent banging on walls hoping they become doors is simply too high. I am here to tell you that the process I give you within the pages of this book works. I had to lead myself through it before

I could lead others. See, you cannot lead people where you have never been. It worked for me in such a way that I came to believe I'd be doing others a disservice by keeping it to myself. You see, God doesn't give us a story so we can keep it to ourselves. He gifts us life so we can serve and help those around us! I was literally compelled to leave my entire career and embark on a journey that I had no qualifications for or experience in. That choice required me to take risks I was absolutely terrified to take and face fears I didn't even know I had in order to make sure you receive this message.

Precious reader, please know that you have a purpose, one that is unique, individual, and is needed by so many people. You are important. You cannot afford to spend one more moment stuck in a stagnant position, especially if it's because of fear.

Your life *is* manageable and you *will* find immense joy and hope for your future after reading the wisdom contained in this book because it is not mine, it is based entirely on the truth and example of Jesus Christ.

Part 1

The Purpose Perspective

Chapter 1
Gratitude

"Gratefulness unlocks the fullness of life. It turns what we have into enough and more. It turns denial into acceptance, chaos to order, confusion to clarity. It can turn a meal into a feast, a house into a home, a stranger into a friend."
– Melody Beattie

T ry to imagine this...

You awake each morning eager to show appreciation for your life. You anxiously await the next opportunity to sprinkle kindness on someone like confetti. You are grounded and able to handle the day's inevitable ups and downs. You are focused and efficient because you are prepared for your daily tasks. You are confident in your ability to handle whatever lies ahead.

Meeting your reflection in the mirror you feel a smile begin to dance at the corner of your lips. You are proud of who stares back at you.

Sounds impossible doesn't it?

It probably sounds to you like a "pretend fairy tale land" where only people who've never witnessed any of life's cruelty live. Or people who don't have as stressful a job as you do. Maybe they have more money or less kids... The list could go on. But what if I told you that the one I just described could be you? The "you" who has harnessed the power of gratitude and enjoys the joy, peace and fulfillment resulting from living out their God-given purpose. The "you" who has claimed their freedom. This is possible and this book can serve as your road map, a step by step guide to take you from where you are to where you want to go.

Gratitude is one of, if not the most influential factors you can have on your life. It is the first and most fundamental piece of the Purpose Perspective, laying the foundation for the rest of the process. Applying this new foundation in your mind will help you to be able to see things differently throughout your day and ultimately your life. But before I lay this process out for you, I need you to do something very important.

Take a moment now, wherever you are, to close your eyes and give yourself permission. Permission to be open to freedom, even if you're not sure what your freedom looks like yet. I believe somewhere deep inside you there is a stirring, compelling you toward 'freedom.' What personal liberty means may be different for each person, but the desire to attain it stays the same. This desire is within all of us. In fact, the United States of America was founded on the very right of "liberty for all." Without knowing it, we can hold ourselves back from experiencing true freedom because we feel unworthy. I'd like to encourage you to use this moment to refuse that belief and accept the opportunity to move forward toward the life God has designed for you to live – one of complete and utter freedom.

What is Gratitude?

Webster's dictionary defines gratitude as "the state of being grateful." (Grateful defined as "feeling or showing an appreciation of kindness".) Google further defines it as "the quality of being thankful; readiness to show appreciation for and to return kindness." I've combined the two as: the state of being ready to show appreciation and return kindness because we are thankful."

To feel grateful you must have something to be thankful for. There is a big difference between having something to be grateful for and realizing you have it. So many of us have completely lost track of the hundreds– even thousands of things we have to be grateful for on a daily basis. We need to overhaul our thinking so that we learn how to be grateful for even the most basic things in life. We need to establish an "attitude of gratitude" so let's begin with one of the most basic human gifts: breath.

When you woke up this morning were you responsible to put the air in your lungs? Did you simply choose to turn on your breathing? No, but someone did. The infinite creator, the Owner of life and death, has gifted you that breath. This is not earned; instead, it's a gift that's freely given. We cannot do anything for it nor are we meant to know the moment it could be taken from us. Every time our lungs fill with air we are given the opportunity to be grateful. The very essence of life itself is a gift. **We are responsible to appreciate that**. Breath is just one of thousands of things we have to be grateful for on a physical level.

Now, how about something non physical: the ability to reason. Did we create our ability to rationalize? No. Did we create our ability to problem solve? No. But we have them. Each time we are faced with a choice, or opportunity to grow we can enlist these abilities to better ourselves. That is an opportunity for gratitude. **We are responsible to appreciate it**. (Exception to take into consideration is someone with a psychotic disorder. Their ability to reason is effected due to faulty sensory input.)

These are examples of ways to train your mind to begin recognizing things to be grateful for that we might otherwise overlook or take for granted. The fact that the very essence of life is a gift illustrates the position that gratefulness should have in our priorities. It is first, our foundation, our home base. It reminds us not to do anything without remembering it was first made possible by a gift from a loving God.

Gratitude and Happiness

I may be the only Personal Development Coach alive that doesn't particularly like modern day Self-Help. Although my passion is showing people how to help themselves, I feel the industry as a whole has taken a detour from certain foundational truths. This is due, in part, to the internet giving a platform for all to share their ideas as fact, contaminating the integrity of information. To be perfectly frank I think most of today's "Self-Help" is complete nonsense.

Here's why...

The American culture, along with several others, is obsessed with happiness. There are actually cultural pressures to "be happy." Naturally, this leads us on a "search to find happiness." The Self-Help industry was created to meet that growing demand with methods believed to be helpful in reaching that goal. Although the tactics may vary, the concept stays the same: focus on yourself. Focus on happiness. Travel within and find the happiness that's waiting for your arrival to that place of self awareness where it resides. You're told time and time again that *"you are worth the life you want,"* and *"you deserve the life of your dreams,"* meant to encourage you to use that sense of entitlement as lasting motivation. This is supposed to start you on your journey towards "obtaining" happiness.

This ideology is very popular because it makes people feel warm and fuzzy inside. The only problem is that it's fundamentally flawed because it presupposes that happiness is an entity which can be obtained.

The philosophy upon which this book is based is two-fold:

First, *I believe happiness is not a goal; it's a result.*

The more priority one places on being happy, the more unhappy they become. The pressure to be happy makes people less happy. Organizing your life around trying to become happier, making happiness the primary objective of life, gets in the way of actually experiencing happiness! By making happiness a goal, you give it independent existence. Instead of being defined as an <u>object to be owned</u>, it's seen as a <u>state of being</u> to be achieved. If you set out to find "happiness" in and of itself, you will end up chasing the elusive butterfly that always remains just out of reach. Instead, I suggest to you that your primary objective should be to make the life choices that would result in happiness– then watch how quickly your joy manifests. I submit that living an intentional life rooted in the foundation of gratitude results in things such as joy, fulfillment, patience, peace, direction, etc. This whole concept speaks to the **motive behind our actions, not the action in and of itself**. (I'll explain this further in a bit...)

Secondly, I believe gratitude is the most important aspect of achieving the fulfilling and successful life you want, because it produces a sense of responsibility to find and live out your purpose. This perspective places gratitude as the lens through which purpose is seen as the only route leading to true fulfillment. It compels us to best utilize the power of choice we all possess. (Don't worry, we'll discuss this more later.)

Both philosophies are so critical to your understanding of the rest of this book that I need to insure you grasp them fully. First, let's illustrate the importance of defining happiness as the result of our choices, not an object to be found.

Lets imagine Suzy...

On an ordinary Wednesday, as she pours her morning coffee, the usual malaise begins to set in. She looks around hopelessly at the never ending pile of dishes in the sink, toys strewn everywhere, piles of laundry washed but not folded, and the dust bunnies that are multiplying before her very eyes like, well, bunnies. She dazes off, reminiscing about what her house once looked like when she had the time to keep it clean. Feelings of overwhelm and despair wash over her as she begins to feel helpless. "How will I ever get this place clean?" she wonders. She finds herself seeking solace by mentally revisiting the place in which she has neatly tucked away all of her "reasons" why she can't keep her house clean on a regular basis anymore. As she begins up the stairs to wake her children, she passes through her living room, family room, stairway, and bathroom– all of which look like a bomb went off. She wishes her home was orderly. She knows how happy and peaceful she would feel if it were clean, and she vaguely remembers a time in which she managed to keep it clean amidst her many other obligations. But again, she tells herself that it's simply impossible. As she enters her youngest child's room, she trips over the fire truck left directly in the doorway and spills the last of her coffee all over the carpet. Exasperated, she starts internally blaming her husband for never helping her. "Where was he anyway? Why doesn't he ever help me?" she mutters. Going about the rest of her day she feels more on edge than usual as she continues to nurse the anger toward her husband.

Let's pause here for a moment. Where is the error in Suzy's thinking? What could she have already done differently to change the course of her day?

Let's take a look at Mary, living across the street that same Wednesday morning...

Pouring her first cup of coffee, Mary faces the mess in her home that's been growing over the past week, or maybe month. She stands for a moment, surveying the damage: dishes piled high, toys strewn about, the laundry she washed but never folded, etc. As she begins to despair at the seemingly impossible task of managing it all, she stops and remembers back to the point in time when she managed to keep an orderly home, even with all her other obligations. "What's changed from then till now?" she asks herself. As she begins up the stairs to wake her children, she passes through the various rooms in her home that also look like a bomb went off. She stops for a moment in each room thinking silently to herself. As she reaches her youngest child's door, she has formulated a plan. She realized that although the entire house was a mess, she couldn't possibly clean it all in one day, nor would she expect herself too. Instead, she would begin room by room taking it a day at a time, until the whole house was completed. She recognized the time this would take and the challenge it presented, but she smiled knowing the result was worth it. The peace that an orderly home would provide her and her family was well worth the effort. As she enters the room, she trips over a fire truck left right at the entrance. Spilling her coffee on the carpet, she shakes her head and chuckles. Quickly realizing her gratefulness for the child that lie sleeping a few feet away. She recognizes the mess in her house represents a home well-lived in and is filled with gratitude.

What's the difference between Suzy and Mary?

On the surface, everything appears the same, but there is a very subtle yet powerful difference between the way these two think. At the foundation of each of their thinking lies a root. One is bitter, producing only bitter fruit; selfishness, discontentment, unhappiness, victimization, disappointment, etc. The other is sweet, bearing the good fruit of: patience, joy, self control, peace, fulfillment, etc. Suzy exposed the root in her mind by the fruit manifested in her life. She is overwhelmed, unhappy and discontent within her circumstance, incorrectly placing responsibility for the solution to her problem onto something else– aka blaming her husband. That poisonous root propagates more bitter fruit by causing her anger. Mary, on the other hand, enjoys the benefit of her good fruits during times of challenge. Her ability to remain grateful places her in a position of control, while Suzy has succumbed to the idea that her circumstances are beyond her control.

The house is analogous to our lives, with each room representing the different areas we must maintain like health, finances, career, relationships, etc. When each compartment of our lives have become disorderly we often resort to overwhelm, despair and hopelessness. Suzy and Mary represent two different paths we can take when presented with life challenges. I believe that gratitude serves as a reminder that your choices are an expression of thankfulness, anchoring you to the reality where they are the most important step in achieving true happiness. Mary took responsibility for creating the solution to her issue, because she understood that although the task at hand seemed impossible– as is easy to feel when life becomes unmanageable, she had a responsibility to make choices that reflected her thankfulness. Ultimately this led her to create a life of purpose that produces the happiness she seeks. That's what gratitude does.

Gratitude and Purpose

Gen Y (current 20's to 30's) has been saturated with the ideas of empowerment and entrepreneurialism. We have been told to want more, be more, do more and have more. We've been led to believe we are capable of achieving more than our predecessors and we take liberties to pursue ALL of our ambitions. We no longer settle for the idea of working a 9-5 for someone else in an office an hour away from home. No. We each want to start our **own** business so we can work from the beach in Tahiti whenever we feel like it! Or, perhaps we aspire to obtain a position within a company that offers certain perks, affording us a lifestyle we desire. Generations before us would have never dared to dream some of the dreams that we do. We are a generation with a lot of chutzpa! We are a generation of empowered thinkers.

Inadvertently, this has led us to believe that our professional accomplishments define our personal success or should be the foundation for our happiness. This could be why we are surrounded by "successful people" who have accomplished what they've set out to achieve but lack the very fulfillment they anticipated. When I was a power player in Corporate America, I came across numerous people who had many notable accomplishments but were visibly unhappy. They invested the majority of their lives into building achievements that may have delivered a handsome paycheck, but certainly not the fulfillment they truly wanted. This indicates a disconnect between our defined success and the presence of fulfillment. (Which is a large contributor to happiness.) I wonder then, why, with all of this empowerment and opportunity, aren't we creating more fulfilled, and content individuals?

I believe I have the answer...

When was the last time you met someone who was confident they were living out their purpose? My whole career has been a case study for this exact question. Based on my experience, I would submit to you that most people, if asked "Do you know what your God given purpose is?" would quickly answer "No". If pressed further they would probably tell you "I don't know what it is, but I want to find it." An article on Theatlantic.com cites a study conducted by the Center for Disease Control in 2010 which concludes that "4 out of 10 Americans have not discovered a satisfying life purpose. Forty percent either do not think their lives have a clear sense of purpose or are neutral about whether their lives have purpose. Nearly half of all Americans feel neutral about or do not have a strong sense of what makes their lives meaningful."

This is alarming, but not surprising. The correlation between lack of purpose and lack of fulfillment becomes obvious. Accomplishment in and of itself does not necessarily indicate the fulfillment of your ultimate purpose. It can deliver you to an empty success—an achievement devoid of meaning. Using Gen Y as a statistical sample, we can deduct that empowerment, inspiration, and achievement alone are not enough to deliver you into a life of fulfillment and subsequent happiness. There must be a root source in which all these things flow from, a centralized hub from which all else is energized.

That source is your God-given purpose!

Logically, you should be led to link your God-given purpose to your ultimate fulfillment.

Multiple studies confirm, along with my own experience, that "having purpose" has numerous benefits on both physical and mental health. Further explanation of this is discussed at length in the next chapter, but remember the focus of this chapter is simply the role gratitude plays in fulfillment.

To conclude, it is by gratitude that we can properly value our purpose to the point in which we decide to discover it and walk it out. Remember earlier when we recognized that the essence of life itself is a gift from God? Well, I believe that that gift has some 'strings attached' to it ...

I believe that although it is a gift that's freely given, it was not meant to be simply accepted and thats it. No, I see immense wisdom in those who understand that it has been given for a reason. That reason being the specific task in which He designed you to fulfill. It is not one universal task, that all humans share. Although I do believe the command to love others and believe in Jesus Christ as your Savior is a universal purpose for all humans. Beyond that, we each possess a singular, individual meaning. That meaning is our purpose, our task, or job, or responsibility to accomplish on this earth. It is uniquely designed to benefit you and others. I believe it is only through sincere and utter acknowledgement of God's design for life that we are able to value the choice we have to either accept or ignore our calling. When we choose to accept it, we live out of the awareness that it is our expression of gratitude to God for all He has done, is doing, and will do in our lives. A choice that ultimately leads us to our true fulfillment.

It's a beautiful, supernaturally designed cycle.

Action Steps

Use these statements to help infuse gratitude into your daily life.

- Today I am thankful that I have the ability to improve myself through discipline.

- Today I am thankful that I am offered forgiveness for my failures and shortcomings.

- I am grateful that no matter what my circumstances are, no one can stop me from loving those around me.

- I am grateful that I have woken up today. Although the day ahead is unknown, I am glad I have the ability to choose my perspective.

- I am grateful for the ways in which I have grown over the past year.

- I am thankful for the hard lessons life has taught me because without them I wouldn't be as strong as I am.

- I am grateful that in a world full of so much darkness I am able to find the light of truth and shine it in my environment.

- Today I am grateful that in the midst of my questions, frustrations, pain, and annoyance I can find peace in the promise that I am never alone.

- I am grateful for the personality I have been given: for my quirks that keep me humble and my strengths that give me confidence.

Chapter 2
Purpose

What Is It?

P urpose is the heart of life. It's the source of energy that produces your passion, gifts and fulfillment. It serves as the central hub from which all those things are produced. Fulfilling your purpose is the most efficient way to experience true lasting joy. It is the vessel in which our meaning is held, leaving the two nearly indistinguishable. A key part to what makes us human is the innate desire to find our meaning. I believe that a meaningful life is significantly more valuable than a happy life. Yet, by finding meaning, happiness inevitably results.

I further define purpose as the task or set of tasks created at the juncture of your gifts and the needs of the world. This can seem elusive but it's actually not. Although every individual's purpose is unique, the process stays the same. Your passion and gift set contain all the information you need in order to discover exactly what you were born to do. A bit later on I will walk you through a step by step explanation of this process but for now, all you need to grasp is a clear understanding of what purpose is.

The importance of identifying and living out your purpose is so enormous I have to break it up into a few basic points...

The Inversion

Picture a tree. It has roots, a trunk, and some branches right? Well, I believe we as individuals mimic the same structure as a tree. Gratitude serves as our root system; dug deeply into the soil, the roots provide a firm foundation for the strong and sturdy trunk to grow. That trunk contains the power source of our purpose; serving as the the backbone of our entire lives. It gives birth to the beautiful branches of passion, gifts and fulfillment. Now add on a lush green leaf that forms off the branch of fulfillment. *That leaf is happiness, just one of the perfect results from the whole magical creation.* (Other results such as contentment, peace, wisdom, love, self control, etc. are produced too, but for relevance to this book I'm speaking only about happiness.) **I believe this order is the original and perfect design for personal development**. It places everything in its correct position thus assigning each its appropriate value. This model should create grounded, grateful, fulfilled and joyful people.

Earlier we outlined the flawed thinking of many modern day societies, (specifically American) in which happiness is created to be an entity with independent existence. This mindset creates an *inversion* that places happiness first and purpose second, making the latter into an afterthought– one we will worry about after we "get happy." This is detrimental to our structure because it creates a hollow root system that's expected to support the weight of our existence.

When inverted, a sort of chaotic swap occurs. Happiness gets placed as the root, becoming our main focus that is valued highest within our lives. Our trunk, the power source from which our meaning is derived, becomes replaced with immediate gratification, compelling us toward self focus and ease. While accomplishments, skills and money become the branches, leaving us chronically discontent, chasing that elusive butterfly.

And we wonder why things are a mess?

People are experiencing despair. Families are falling apart, and societies as a whole are regressing in more ways than one. That is not coincidental or unavoidable.

I strongly believe it is due to the acceptance of this inversion as truth. It creates a model that is dependent on a hollow root system. Happiness is then not only misdefined but placed as the entire foundation upon which all else is dependent. This is why, as we saw earlier, the more you pursue happiness the more unobtainable it becomes. It was never designed to produce itself or exist independently; it was designed to be a result. When positioned incorrectly, it cannot create anything other than self centered focus. Furthermore, take notice that nowhere in the inversion is gratitude present at all. (Try and find a place where it fits!)

Too often I speak to people who reveal that they see gratitude as an addon. Being "grateful" is something deemed as a spiritual expression reserved for those existing in a realm where it is assumed and no longer seen as a choice. We know from the first chapter the crucial role that gratitude holds in the ability to value purpose. So without that, we are left vulnerable to a lack of direction, becoming lost and 'stuck'. This is the result of gratitude becoming an afterthought, as opposed to the main focus of everything we do, every day of our lives.

It saddens me deeply to see so many lives play out the consequences of this inverted thinking. Especially when it is likely due to ignorance that things could be better (and should be better). It is my sincerest hope that by painting a clear picture of the originally designed structure God intended us to maintain, the incorrect inversion will become exposed and corrected, restoring truth back into peoples lives.

Secondly, I believe we, as unique and individual human beings, bear a responsibility to understand that our purpose holds impact not just for us, but for others too. Research suggests that people who identify a "meaning" for their lives can endure even the worst of circumstances. This understanding brings magnitude to the accountability we have not only to ourselves but to life itself, to fulfill our purpose for those who may need what only we can offer. This thought is not original; it is accepted by many experts in both the psychological and theological fields.

My favorite example is Viktor Frankl. A holocaust survivor in the 1940's, Frankl went on to write one of the top 10 most influential books in the United States called Man's Search For Meaning. He was a neurologist and psychiatrist by trade and worked as a therapist in the camps during his imprisonment. In his book, he gives the example of two suicidal inmates he encountered while in the camp. Like many others there, these two men were hopeless and thought that there was nothing more to expect from life, nothing to live for. "In both cases," Frankl writes, "it was a question of getting them to realize that life was still expecting something from them; something in the future was expected of them." For one man, it was his young child, who was then living in a foreign country. For the other, a scientist, it was a series of books that he needed to finish. Frankl writes:

"This uniqueness and singleness which distinguishes each individual and gives a meaning to his existence has a bearing on creative work as much as it does on human love. When the impossibility of replacing a person is realized, it allows the responsibility which a man has for his existence and its continuance to appear in all its magnitude. A man who becomes conscious of the responsibility he bears toward a human being who affectionately waits for him, or to an unfinished work, will never be able to throw away his life. He knows the "why" for his existence, and will be able to bear almost any "how."

Frankl so perfectly explains the truth that is too often overlooked or unknown to begin with. Comprehending that our purpose holds relevance beyond ourselves creates a responsibility, motivation, and duty to fulfill it. This is the ideology upon which

Selfless Development is built. (More on this later...)

Real Life Example...

When I was 19, I enrolled in a local community college to begin studying psychology. I always found people intriguing, so it seemed the logical choice. I quickly learned I was quite possibly the worst student alive. I had done well in high school, but was entirely disinterested when it came to college. So one semester, after skipping all of my finals, I decided to drop out. I figured if I couldn't take the commitment seriously, why waste my own money? At that point, all I wanted to do was work. I just wanted freedom and independence.

Now during these few months, I was going through a break up with my high school sweetheart, whom I had been dating for 3 years fully intending to marry. This rendered my previously anticipated future a blank slate. Since my heart hurt from that and other difficult family situations, I was highly motivated to make a safe choice. So, through whatever rationale I used at the time, I decided I wanted to be a business woman.

(I think its important to note here, the influence my personal life had on my professional choice. Many times we fail to realize the influence each part of our lives has on the other. We think we can isolate

things that we actually cannot.)

I envisioned being a beautiful, fierce, and powerful CEO, living in a penthouse apartment with a closet full of black pencil skirts and expensive stilettos. I imagined my future self to be financially successful, hold a place of authority at work, and be generally emotionless (which I mistakenly saw as strong). That was the identity that felt good when I tried it on. So, I resolved deeply and fully to become that woman I dreamed of.

I set out to begin this journey by moving as close to New York City as I could afford, which looked like the spare room in my big brother's Hoboken apartment. After scheduling my very first interview at a company in the heart of Manhattan, I got so nervous that I made my sister come with me. I was interviewing for an Executive Assistant position and I had never even been in an office before. But it was my door and I would walk through it. Leaving my sister to wait in the lobby, I made my way to the 11th floor. My palms were sweating and I was almost 30 minutes early. As the receptionist told me to have a seat, I looked around taking in what I hoped would be my new office.

Suddenly, in walked Erez, the Chairman to whom I would assist. His presence alone elicited respect. He was simultaneously intimidating and inspiring. His demeanor was strong yet kindness shown through his eyes, instantly putting me at ease. Before me stood the man whose influence on my life rivals that of my own parents. He would later become a friend as close as a brother, to whom my admiration runs deep.

He hired me on the spot.

The next 7 years, I spent growing and advancing within that company. I earned my first promotion within just 2 months. My investment reached far beyond the expected 9-5. I worked endless hours regardless of expectation, learned new positions when the company required it, relocated twice, traveled the globe at a week's notice, sacrificed my personal life, cried from frustration and feelings of inadequacy, and struggled to succeed when I was given responsibilities for which I was underqualified.

But I never quit. I never gave up.

I held a deep sense of responsibility to both myself and Erez to succeed. More times than not, his belief in me outweighed my own– a gift I did not take for granted. I was determined to become that beautiful power player I envisioned... no matter what.

Fast-forward now to 5 years later, on a dreary day in a corner office in London. Stunned, I sat across from Erez trying to absorb his last statement.

Me? Sit on the Board of Directors?

"I cannot possibly do that. I am not ready. I am underqualified. I am 24! How? Why?" I rambled.

"You'll be fine, Kristin. I believe in you. You're also being made partner." He replied.

In that moment I experienced a sense of unprecedented personal achievement. I was officially a respected business woman and had the title to prove it. I had actually done it.

As expected, the title I now bore as the Director of Compliance came with a new level of commitment to the company, but I didn't mind the sacrifice. For the next 2 years, I continued my move up the corporate ladder, gaining new levels of experience and respect in my field. I faced many difficult challenges but always forged my way through.

Then suddenly, a personal tragedy struck that stopped me dead in my tracks.

My marriage of nearly 3 years abruptly ended. Although we loved each other deeply, the consequence for certain choices that were made changed the course of both our lives forever. Within just 6 short months I was divorced and devastated. The shock was as difficult to handle as the loss itself, so I can't tell you which to attribute more pain to. The next 18 months were a downward spiral into a darkness I'd never known before, one that seemed to rise from the bottom of my soul like a silent snake choking the very life from my being. The toxic mix of pain, loss, guilt, and shame sent me into a space designated only for the fragmented. The few nights where sleep didn't evade me, I would wake with what felt like a 20 lb. weight on my chest. I had previously faced a lot of challenges in life, but this season taught me some of life's hardest lessons.

Allow me to pause here, drawing attention to an important point.

I still had a thriving, successful career from which I derived what I believed to be fulfillment and meaning. It gave me financial stability to live the lifestyle I wanted, respect among my peers, and a deep sense of pride at my accomplishments. I loved my career deeply for all those reasons and it had consumed almost all of my identity. I believed I was fulfilled. I had created a life that contained exactly what I thought I needed to be happy and successful. Yet, when my personal life experienced a breakdown, I was left standing on quicksand. I had no foundation to which I could anchor myself amidst the storm. I had all I believed I was "supposed" to have, yet the moment things went wrong I was left frantic, lost, confused, angry, and rapidly approaching despair. For me, it was the failure of my marriage. But the truth is it wouldn't have mattered what part of my life collapsed because all it would have exposed was my contaminated root system.

I was victim of the inverted tree.

Now, let's resume the story..

After reaching rock bottom, I embarked upon an amazing journey of redemption and healing. God, in His infinite graciousness, had already been positioning all of my failures and successes into a pathway leading me straight to my ultimate destination: my purpose. He restored my dignity and gave me hope again for a bright and joyful future. His restoration of my heart is a story so powerful I cannot commit it to only a few lines. So, for sake of brevity, I just need you to understand that its magnitude is evidenced through the depth of thankfulness it produced in my heart.

As wholeness returned to my life, I found myself

craving a way to say "thank you." I entered a period of soul cleansing where I purged my life of most material and mental distractions that were occupying my time. This created a lot of empty space in which I spent time alone with my mind and God. Through the silence, I started actually hearing the thoughts that pulsed through my mind, day in and day out. Some were good, some were bad, but all of them seemed foreign to me. It was as if I had landed on a frequency in which a stranger was talking. The more I listened, the more light was shed on the mistruths I had been believing for years. I saw that I had accepted the "inversion" as truth and witnessed its failure firsthand.

At the time, I knew nothing of the correct order in which things were supposed to be, but I determined to find it. I had no where else to start other than the craving to express my gratitude, which compelled me more and more toward discovering my purpose. It felt like the most appropriate outlet I had to encompass the fullness of my desire. God had created me, protected me and redeemed me. It seemed like the very least I could do was whatever He created me for. I started remembering what my natural, most innate talents were, realizing quickly that these were my *gifts*. Some were partially developed, others I had completely forgotten. I began discovering connections between what I was naturally good at and what I felt inclined to pursue, arriving at a conclusion that had been there all along. I was passionate about helping people learn how to better themselves and my gifts gave me the abilities to succeed at it. I came to believe that I was born to do something specific and an equation became too obvious to ignore:

Passion + Gifts + Needs of the World = Purpose.

My passion was intended to give me the desire to do what I was naturally gifted at. And best yet, someone out there needed what only I could offer.

I had identified my purpose.

The Freedom Formula

My own experience led me to formulate a process which others could use as a guide to help discover their own purpose. This process is, what I call, "The Freedom Formula" which I will share with you now. But before I do, it's important you know this concept is not something I can take credit for nor should it be attributed solely to common sense or logic. My intent is to present certain truths that originate from the Bible in a way that's simple enough to apply to our everyday lives. I believe (and is the premise of this book) that the word of God is the only source from which all truth, life, and hope are derived. I believe He is the creator of perfect order and it's only by His ability that our actions have meaning. I will discuss this more later, but for now, let me explain the process.

I've simplified it to the following 3 steps:

Step 1. Be Quiet.

> *"God speaks in the silence of the heart.*
> *Listening is the beginning of the prayer."*
> *- Mother Teresa*

The biggest misconception people have about "finding their purpose" is that they must search long and hard for it, as if it somehow went somewhere. I would encourage you to understand that your task is not to look for it, it is to stop ignoring it. Assuming you feel unsure as to what your purpose looks like, the best route to take is to identify and remove whatever is preventing you from connecting with your base, natural inclinations. I call these *drives*. Now, there's a difference between drives and desires. I believe desires indicate a pull toward something that results in a benefit to self or ego. Drive is what we are created to be ambitious about, regardless of who it benefits. This is most effectively done by silencing the external distractions in your life so you can see what's really going on inside yourself.

I want you to picture the sun on a beautiful summer's day. The sky is free of clouds leaving you wrapped in its warmth and radiance. There is nothing but fresh air between you and it. Your line of sight is completely unobstructed. But then, some clouds roll in, bringing with them sheets of rain. The downpour becomes so strong that you can barely see through it. The sun that was once so clear is now hidden by the clouds and rain.

This is what happens when we allow distractions to accumulate in our lives, occupying most of our time and energy. Our purpose becomes hidden under the mass of other things we have prioritized higher. It never went anywhere or changed; it just got buried.

I define a distraction as: any exertion or consumption of energy that does not contribute to an intentional outcome. This can take many different forms depending on the individual. There is no set list of "no-no's" that I can give you because it doesn't exist. You must look carefully at your daily life and determine what is advancing you toward a goal and what is a waste of your time. Whatever distractions you identify– remove them. The time left in their absence will need to be used wisely.

Leading us to...

Step 2. Identifying your gifts.

When you were born, you were entrusted with a set of natural abilities or tendencies. These are your gifts. There are several key differences between skills and gifts and it's important to properly differentiate the two. Skills are learned; while, gifts are innate. They both require development, but the process will be different.

Let me give you an example to insure you understand the difference...

Sally begins a job as a chef because she needs a night job to get through college. She learns how to cook what's on the menu because thats what's required to fulfill the job. She performs her work in exchange for a paycheck. At the end of her shifts she normally leaves feeling drained, dirty, and exhausted.

Contrast that with a child named Nate, who at the age of 6 can always be found in the kitchen. Most nights he just wants to sit watching dinner be made. He is fascinated by every detail of food. For Christmas, he wants a toy kitchen. In high school, he elects for cooking class, immediately dreaming up dishes the teacher didn't assign! Upon finishing culinary school, he becomes a chef at his dream restaurant. He gets paid in exchange for his expertise. At the end of his shifts he normally leaves feeling accomplished, energized, and grateful.

At the end of the day both Sally and Nate are Chefs. Yet, Sally only developed a skill while Nate utilized his gift.

Gifts are exertions of energy that leave you feeling energized, not drained. These are the abilities, tendencies, and inclinations you feel naturally within your soul. By identifying them, you are positioned perfectly to begin step 3....

Step 3. Discover your passion.

The English word "passion" originates from the Latin word "Patoir" which means "to suffer or endure." It evolved to mean "the very strong emotion that sustains the one who suffers." ***It is not coincidental that passion is the substance of perseverance.***

And here is why...

Your purpose will be a task that hangs delicately in the balance of attainable and unreachable. By its very nature, it will require you to face whatever will make you stronger. Your comfort zone is not big enough to contain the wonder within your purpose! You are perfectly equipped with the raw materials needed to carry out your purpose; however, the development of those materials is what requires faith, foresight, discipline, grit, perseverance and an unwavering commitment to the cause.

That is passion.

I enjoy seeing different success stories of people who have defied the odds to arrive at success and renown– people like Steve Jobs, Mother Theresa and Oprah Winfrey. These specific stories can help us bridge the gap between the people we see as "superior" to us and the "normal" simple beings we identify as. They represent people who are just like us, but have somehow succeeded wildly.

How did they do it? Why did they do it? What made them "get it" and how do you get that same result? Well, let's start with what they had to say for themselves:

> *"Follow your passion, it will lead you*
> *to your purpose."*
> *– Oprah Winfrey*

"You have to have a lot of passion for what you are doing, because it is so hard... If you don't, any rational person would give up."
– Steve Jobs

"We must know that we have been created for greater things, not just to be a number in the world. Not just to go for diplomas and degrees, this work and that work. We have been created in order to love and to be loved."
– Mother Teresa

People who have accessed passion can face insurmountable odds and beat them because whatever they do as a result of that passion is an expression of meaning– a creation of their purpose. The fire burning inside is motivation enough to develop whatever is needed to accomplish the task. They see a challenge and overcome it. They don't back down because they can't, something deep down inside will not let them. It is not a fear of failure; it is a need to accomplish the greater good.

Discovering this is based on self awareness and honesty. Believe it or not, there can be a hesitation to accept what you feel is your passion. There are sometimes different experiential, cultural, or societal influences on what you deem "appropriate" or "acceptable" to pursue. This can cause an internal judgment to occur, preventing you from embracing your true calling. One key way to identify your passion is to ask yourself the question, "Would I still want to do this if I didn't get paid?" If the answer is no, you must keep looking. If the answer is yes, you have landed on a task or set of tasks, which you would pursue regardless of money or fame or ease. There will be a sense of peace that washes over you as you accept that direction, and resolve to pursue it.

In conclusion, don't be surprised if you have several different passions. Although I believe our purpose is somewhat singular, it is the hub from which many different passions grow. Some of which may apply to your profession (what you do to make money), while others may be personal (only affecting yourself). You may have a passion for something that will be used to benefit those who can never repay you, compensate you or thank you. All of these are likely. So, don't limit yourself to believing you can only have one, or that some are more important than others.

Action Steps

Freedom Formula Recap
    Step 1. Be Quiet
    Step 2. Identify Your Gifts
    Step 3. Discover Your Passion(s)

- Write down 10 things you loved doing before the age of 10.
  (ex: writing, being outside, talking to a friend, acting, etc)

- Write down 5 things that come naturally to you.
  (Ex: problem solving, creativity, helping others, noticing the quiet one in the room, etc)

- Write down 5 things that energize you.
  Hint* This could be something physically draining in the moment, but emotionally fulfilling in the end.

Part 2

The Application Process

Chapter 3
Sustainability

T his is a pivotal time to recap the amazing system that we've uncovered thus far, because we're about to take a bit of a turn.

The first two chapters set the foundation for a pretty huge perspective shift, creating what I call *The Purpose Perspective* ("TPP"). Seeing the common ways in which happiness is misunderstood and misplaced gave us the chance to correct some misguided thinking. We now understand the order in which things were originally intended to be, demonstrated through our tree analogy. When all we are and all we aspire to be is rooted in gratitude to God, we begin to properly value our purpose. Since we were designed to operate this way, our soul helps us along by giving us a desire to find meaning – a desire to fulfill our destiny. Our passion(s) provides us with a powerful compass that points us in a specific direction by drawing us toward certain things and away from others. Not only does it guide us but it gives us the lasting motivation that we need to persevere through our life long journey to fulfillment. Our gifts – the abilities we are naturally given, are the exact resources we need in order to succeed. This perspective greatly affects how we view our specific role in the world, bringing us to a state of awareness that we *matter*; we matter greatly. Everything about us is important and needed. We exist for a reason. Not only does our existence affect us but it is deeply relevant to the operation of the world as a whole.

If that doesn't excite you, nothing will! You may want to reread that last paragraph one more time and really let it sink in, because this is truly an amazing, empowering, and inspiring revelation.

Accomplishment vs. Character

With this understanding, we can begin to look at how this revelation impacts our daily lives. When The Purpose Perspective (TPP) is applied, its effect on personal development is tremendous. One of the greatest areas of impact will be the way you treat yourself. After having identified with a purpose for your life, especially knowing it affects others, you tend to take accountability for yourself in a new way. You are more inclined to take ownership of what you become, because you understand the significance of the character you're creating. A sense of intention and foresight visits your decision making when you realize how much is dependent upon you growing into who you were destined to be!

This is the very essence of selfless development. **It is what occurs when you choose to develop yourself from the mindset that your success it not for your own benefit, but for others.** You are aware that your God-given purpose carries implication far beyond your own gain into the realm of effecting other peoples lives. You begin realizing that your success is uncompromisable because **others** need what only you can offer and God has given you the opportunity to meet that need. The reward you are given is complete fulfillment, peace of mind, and endless joy. Who you are, what you do, and why you do it is no longer relevant only to yourself, but to your legacy and the world. The power of choice becomes such a major asset because through it, you have the ability to direct your life, turning your daily choices into the stepping stones on the path taking you somewhere you're excited to go!

The Importance Of Character

What I love most about living life from this vantage point is that it shifts your focus from accomplishment to character. *You no longer measure your personal success by the sum of your achievements but by the quality of your character.* You begin to recognize that the real challenge in this life is **to become** the best human being you can be, not **to do** the greatest things.

This is a huge change!

Imagine for a moment, if this was the priority of those who surround you, communities filled with individuals determined to become pillars of virtuous character.

What would our world look like?

I dare to dream that its impact would reach far beyond the individuals' quality of life and into the behavior of societies as a whole. The reality is that we are living in a day and age where senseless killings occur every day, worldwide. <u>ABC News reports</u> that "Each week, nearly 60,000 children in the United States are reported as abused or neglected, with nearly 900,000 confirmed abuse victims in 2004. Approximately 800,000 children every year come in contact with the foster care system." One out of every 12 high school students attempt suicide every year. I won't even get into the statistics of commercially sex trafficked women and children worldwide or the rising rates of homelessness and addiction because the list goes on and on, with each statistic more disturbing than the last. What all of this shows us is that we are in the midst of several human crises that mandate we address the deterioration of basic human behavior. But wait, what precedes behavior? From which foundation is behavior cultivated?

Character

Regardless of what your political or religious opinions may suggest as a solution for today's world problems, you cannot deny the one thing they all have in common: **people**. I imagine that this would lead any intelligent observer to realize the deepest most profound battle we face and have always faced, is against the collapse of the human character. I am disappointed and almost disgusted at the extent to which this is neglected within most of today's "Self-Help" approaches. As we saw in Chapter 1, too many of us are lost in some faraway fairy tale land, being taught to chase the elusive "happiness butterfly" instead of being told some of the cold hard truths that would mandate we get our act together. Likewise, some others spend significant time condemning governmental bodies, political parties or religious institutions for agendas that they believe are responsible for the brokenness in our world forgetting that each is comprised of individual people, with individual characters. So, why not start there?

Am I claiming that all world problems will be solved if more people focused on selfless development of character? Not entirely, because some aspects of our humanity are immutable, like free will. But, I absolutely believe there is an urgent need for each individual to understand the role *he/she* plays in affecting positive change. Instead of feeling as though our role is insignificant, it should be seen as invaluable! Each person is carrying a tiny piece (their piece) of the solution. This is real empowerment. It takes any global issue and breaks it down to attainable bits, leaving each person responsible to grow their own character through selfless awareness of its influence on the whole.

That is how we change the world. But don't take my word for it, take Teddy's:

"Character is, in the long run, the decisive factor in the life of individuals and of nations alike."
– Theodore Roosevelt

Character Building 101

"You cannot dream yourself into a character. You must hammer and forge yourself into one."
- Henry David Thoreau

So, what does character building look like? How do you build your character? I believe it takes place right there within your day-to-day life. All those small, trivial moments you may tend to overlook– those are actually crucial. Those are the ones you need to start paying very close attention to, because whether you realize it or not, they are shaping who you are. So, let's talk about the top three essential character building skills you can start to develop immediately. Each one begins as a skill in need of development but should end up becoming a habit over time.

1. Self Honesty

As a Personal Development Coach, I have the pleasure of working with all kinds of clients ranging in age, ethnicity, gender, background and anything else you could name. Each one brings a unique set of strengths and struggles to the table, making my job very interesting. I truly enjoy the challenge presented by their diversity, because a "one-size-fits-all" approach certainly does not work. Despite their uniqueness, however, I find that they all seem to share one thing in common: the struggle to be honest *with themselves about themselves*. I call this a lack of self honesty. This can be a result of internal "defenses" that are both conscious and unconscious. They sincerely do not know who they are because they are unaware of the truth. (We will talk about why in a moment.) When I ask them simple questions like: "What do you like about yourself?" or "What's your greatest strength?" I am met with a searching stare. I'd love to believe that indicates a lack of self awareness in general, presenting me with a blank slate on which I can begin writing how wonderful they are! But that's rarely the case. There is always some type of belief system already in place, so it becomes a matter of whether or not it's truthful. Where self honesty is lacking, there is inevitably the presence of illusions or inaccurate self beliefs that are causing them great harm.

If there are illusions or self manipulations present, it is usually unintentional. I have yet to meet someone who wakes up and willfully determines to be something less than honest with themselves. But nonetheless, it occurs– preventing them from being able to really become who they want to be. This is most likely why they are struggling with the things that led them to hire me in the first place (feeling stuck, discouraged, confused, directionless, etc.). Without an accurate understanding of who they are, my hands are tied, making it very difficult to get them where they want to go. So, my main objective becomes guiding them to discover the truth about who they really are. I do this by introducing "self honesty" into their thought processes, which is the pinnacle area where the truth needs to start. (For sake of brevity, I will refer to self honesty with "honesty" going forward.)

Why is Honesty Important?

Personal growth is fundamentally reliant on the accuracy of our self reflection. What honesty does is allow us to see things as they really are, not as we think they should or shouldn't be. Often times there are big differences between the way we wish something was and the way it is. The best way to differentiate this is through applying objective honesty. We are complex beings possessing both emotional and intellectual intelligence, making us dynamic and alive. Over the span of our lives, we are continually evolving which makes self discovery a truly lifelong journey. This is part of what makes self reflection so beautiful! There is always something new to see. This is why we must stay vigilant in our self reflection because if not, we can easily fall behind, operating with an outdated version of ourselves. It is only through **honest** self assessment that we are able to paint a truthful picture of who we are. This includes our strengths and weaknesses.

Often, we shy away from this honest self assessment out of fear of what we might find; however, that mindset is so backward! I want you to begin picturing self reflection as a form of self care. You learn to look at who you are with acceptance and grace, knowing that the only way you can truly grow is to strengthen your weaknesses and build on your strengths. You cannot do this if you don't know what either of those things are. When you see honesty from this understanding, it becomes like a hug you give yourself, not a punishment.

Why We Create Illusions

Self honesty is a skill that develops with use. The more you do it, the easier it becomes, eventuating as a habit. It's like a muscle. If you don't use it, you lose it. Because it is a skill and not an instinct, we have to *intentionally* choose to use it. If we don't, we are at risk of self manipulation. A bit later on, I will give further explanation of this point discussing the relevance of subconscious belief on our conscious thoughts. But for now, it's important to understand that the mere **lack of** self honesty creates a space that must be occupied by something else. This typically becomes filled with inaccurate illusions.

Furthermore, I submit to you that certain aspects of our culture backhandedly discourage objective self honesty, such as social media. Albeit entertaining, it typically presents a manipulated version of someone's life while claiming to be authentic. I don't imagine that to be a debatable point, but if you feel like that is, think about it from a very basic point of view. A photo taken of someone at home in their pajamas on a "cozy Saturday night" usually gets photoshopped to remove the acne, smooth the skin, slim the waist and fix the lighting before it actually gets posted. As an innocent viewer, all you see is a photo of what appears to be a person lounging at home on a Saturday night, looking impeccably beautiful. This manipulation is very sneaky and subtle but is there nonetheless. As we expose ourselves to this, we are accepting these tiny illusions as reality, a few hundred times a day. (I want you to reread that last sentence.)

Over time this has a significant impact on our ability to notice or value authenticity. If you are a person truly trying to prioritize self honesty, do you see the issue here? At first, the effect of social media on our daily lives may seem very small, but I firmly believe it is poisoning our ability to remain objective about ourselves and others. Objectivity and self honesty go hand in hand. Without honesty you can't remain objective, and without objectivity you struggle to remain honest. The two are integral to understanding yourself. What often happens is that you understand the illusions you have created of yourself and accept them as an actual understanding of who you are, but it is not. You cannot understand something you haven't even seen or something that is distorted. It becomes like looking at something, in this case yourself, through a kaleidoscope. Sure, you see an image, but it certainly isn't accurate.

The reasons why our self image can become distorted by illusions are nearly innumerable because we all think so differently. Sometimes we can prefer to live with our illusions if they're more comforting than our reality. Maybe they're less painful or easier to accept. Maybe we are too scared to face what or who we have become or who we have failed to become. Perhaps it's our upbringing, which conditioned us to carry certain "norms" or "standards" into adulthood which we fail to meet. Maybe it results from religious expectations we fall short of. Cultural influences can also lead us to believe certain things are better or worse than others. Often times it can result from experiencing a trauma that leaves us fragmented from the pain. The list goes on... But I submit to you that regardless of why the illusions are there, if you are truly determined to better yourself and develop a character you are proud of, it begins and ends with your internal honesty. From there, all else is built.

How To Identify Illusions

Do you recall the first step of "The Freedom Formula"? It was to "Be Quiet." This directive is not so much about what you are to *stop* doing, but what you are to *start* doing. Listen to your thoughts. Most times you end up listening only to the feelings that come from your thoughts, instead of the thoughts themselves. This is the perfect place to begin exercising your "honesty" muscle. Simply observe your own mind without judgment, so you can hear what is really going on.

Albeit simple, it is not easy. This concept is primary to several practices in different cultures and religions. The methods of application vary but, the core concept remains the same: listen and observe. Perhaps it's most predominantly associated with the practice of meditation. Through this practice, you are taught to observe your thoughts **without trying to change them**. What I adore about this method is that you are not told to fill the time with any other objective than observation. Sit, listen, observe, repeat. It's beautiful. You are not told to try and change what you hear but simply become aware of it by deciding to listen. I don't believe the practice of quieting yourself in order to hear your thoughts has any spiritual implication in and of itself. I believe it is a significantly beneficial act that can and will benefit anyone of any belief system. However, if coupled with the request for God to help you see beyond your own understanding, you create an opportunity for *personal* and *spiritual* growth. (Two birds with one stone!) By revealing His wisdom in unison with your thoughts, He can accelerate your growth and awareness, making this time an especially enlightening experience.

Now, listening is not quite enough. So, let's look at what to do with what you hear...

The study of subconscious thought fills a robust body of psychological research. Specifically, studies often focus on the ways in which the subconscious mind influences our conscious thoughts. This topic alone comprises over a century of focused research. So, keeping in mind it is a complex discussion, I will touch on just one small part that I believe is relevant to my point.

As everyday people, not trained in psychology, it's

easy to misunderstand a very important reality about our thoughts. First, let's define conscious thoughts as the ones we are aware of and subconscious thoughts being the ones occurring in the background. Often times, we make decisions based on rationale involving only our conscious thoughts, omitting the secondary decision that was also made. This happens because we tend to credit our conscious thoughts as whole, independent entities carrying a singular, straight forward message. This leads us to believe that the message/thought we are aware of is the only one bearing influence on our actions. In other words, we believe that awareness of our conscious thoughts is enough to make informed decisions regarding our well being. This is not the case at all.

From that vantage point we've given almost no credence to the subconscious influence (or secondary message) that is also present. When was the last time you listened to one of your thoughts and said to yourself "Hold on. I wonder what my subconscious had to do with that?"

Likely never.

It's imperative to account for the subconscious influence our thoughts are under, because whether we realize it or not, they bear great influence on our belief system and the choices we make. Since I know this concept can be a lot to take in, allow me to use an analogy to better illustrate my point...

Imagine you've been selected to interview for a potential promotion. It's for a position that would definitely challenge you. As your appointment approaches, you wrestle with feelings of intimidation and doubt. You decide to read back over the job description and this time you realize you aren't nearly proficient enough in several of the needed tasks and you begin to feel inadequate. You know with time you could be reasonably qualified, but suddenly fear begins to take over. Your conscious thoughts may look something like this, *"I'm not going to get the job. I know I'm not. They are going to see I'm under-qualified and decide to go with someone better. I know Theresa's interviewing too, and she's a lot more experienced than I am. Why am I even interviewing at all? It's going to be so embarrassing if I don't get it. What was I thinking?"* So, you decide not to interview.

Now let's tune into the potential core self beliefs that are fueling those thoughts,

"I'm not good enough. I'm not smart enough. I will not succeed. This rejection will break me. Choose safely because danger is ahead."

Considering only your conscious thoughts, a decision not to interview may seem the best route. But, when considering the deeper self beliefs at play, I submit to you that your decision will have a significant impact on your self-esteem. Deciding not to interview may be a way of affirming that all those statements are true! This ultimately reinforces the belief that you really aren't smart enough or that you don't deserve success because you're not strong enough to step up to the plate.

This is heart breaking!

Listening let's us recognize the first part— the conscious thoughts. The second task is to account for the subconscious influence(s) they may be under. This is not as scary or as hard as it sounds, but it does only come with practice and objectivity. Honesty becomes such an asset because it allows us to listen to ourselves without judgment, exposing what our underlying belief systems actually are. It places us in the position to acknowledge the negative self beliefs and remove them, making us stronger than ever. Then we can make truly informed decisions that care for our whole self.

I hope you see now why self honesty is so essential in cultivating a realistic and positive self image. Without it, we could be (and almost always are) affirming so many negative beliefs without even realizing it. So, the best place to start is by learning how to be quiet and observe. The more aware we become of our conscious thoughts, the more aware we can become of the hidden ones.

This is one of the top reasons why quality, professional coaching provides such substantial benefits to people. I achieve significant results for my clients, because as an objective outsider I listen to what you say and play back the version you didn't realize you said, gradually showing you how to do the same. (Honesty to the rescue yet again!)

In conclusion, self honesty is integral to the development of character because it establishes your starting point: who you are now. It helps you become aware of your self beliefs in order to remove the negatives and build on the positives. From there you can determine who you want to become and how to get there.

2. The Excuse Filter

Whenever we set out to meet goals, we will inevitably encounter road blocks along the way. These are the challenges that occur within our circumstance(s) that cause us delay. They can range from a minor speed bump to a major road closure. The ability to properly classify these challenges into their rightful place is a determining factor between those that *try* and those that *do*. What happens most often, is that people misunderstand the difference between a reason and an excuse, wrongfully classifying excuses as legitimate reasons. The result of this is that we end up turning what is really just a speed bump *into* a complete road closure, causing us unnecessary and avoidable delay. After I show you just how toxic excuses are to your life, you will not be able to live without your Excuse Filter. It is a skill specifically designed to help you identify and remove excuses from your life. It is one of my favorite points in this entire book because it determines the measure of control we either have or give away, regarding our future. The people that grasp this concept in its entirety are the unstoppable forces that end up changing the world.

Reasons vs. Excuses

Our working definition of a "reason" is: a legitimate circumstance that is out of your control which involves accountability being appropriately assigned among any & all parties involved.

Our working definition for an "excuse" is: an explanation of a circumstance that aims to place the blame for your own actions, or the subsequent result of them, onto something else.

What's the main difference?

Accountability.

A reason is a circumstance that is out of your control while an excuse is largely your choice. It's important to specify the difference between *responsibility* and *accountability*; responsibility can be shared while accountability cannot. Being accountable includes being responsible for something, but also implies being answerable for your actions. (This is a key point!) Accountability is something you hold a person to only after a task is done or not done. Responsibility can be before and/or after a task. When we take accountability for our role in something we are actually acknowledging that we have an element of control. If there was no control, there would be no responsibility for which we need to answer. To acknowledge control means you had/have it.

As this concept is targeted toward goal achievement, it becomes a life saver to the control freak. I speak from experience because this was a breakthrough revelation in my own life. Being a naturally driven and ambitious woman, I have always struggled with patience (and that's putting it nicely). During the earlier years of my career, while my experience and knowledge were still being built, I was consistently frustrated when faced with an issue that I couldn't resolve on my own. This meant I had to wait on someone or something that inevitably took longer than I wanted them to. I felt like I didn't have the resources to move forward without my superior's insight or expertise (or whatever the case may have been), so I found myself waiting a lot. This was difficult for me because I felt powerless to complete my task and it hung over me like an unfinished sentence. The inaction drove me nuts, but it was actually during the times that I was forced to pause that my brain searched for other solutions. If there was a way to move forward without whomever it was that I needed, I was determined to find it. By doing this, I began to see that I actually had way more resources within my control than I had previously realized. If I had just used them better, I could have minimized my wait time. Sure, it was much easier to wait for someone else to fix the problem, but I wasn't interested in easy. I was interested in control because that was how I could move forward. This ended up reclassifying some previously labeled "road closures" into the "speed bump" category, restoring control back into my hands! When I tasted that reality, I began to feel as though there was no limit to what I could achieve.

I spend most of my days as a coach listening to unsatisfied people expressing why their lives seem to be "stuck" in a place they don't like. Occasionally, they are facing some actual barriers, but most of the time they have halted in front of a pebble believing it's a boulder. My heart breaks when I see how powerless this misperception renders them; however, it is equally as heartwarming to watch their eyes light up as the truth restores the possibility of moving forward. There are inevitably reasons we run into that can cause us unavoidable delay, but these are so scarce that they are almost inconsequential. I prefer to have the mindset that **there is always a solution to a problem, it's just a matter of finding or creating it**. So, the challenge here is to begin recognizing excuses before they cause damage. When our minds are conditioned to be honest and objective, identifying and removing excuses becomes a lot simpler. That's why this is skill #2, not #1.

(Isn't it cool how each piece of this process paves the way for the next? That's how things are supposed to work when operating in perfect order!)

How To Recognize Excuses

Begin by analyzing the explanation you give as to why you can't meet a certain goal. It's usually riddled with justifications, a.k.a excuses, disguised as reasons. So, in order to differentiate between the two, you have to apply *The Excuse Filter*. I find that, typically, excuses will fit into three different categories. Think of them like different identities, each with an individual rationale. If your "reason" fits into one of these categories, it's likely an excuse.

Category 1: The Victim

This is when the cause of your inability to accomplish what you want is always due to something you can't change.

> "I don't have enough money." (to start that business you've been dreaming of...)
> "There's never enough time to go to the gym." (when complaining about your weight...)
> "There are no good men out there." (as you sit lonely at home.)
> "My house can never stay clean, it's just too small." (as you trip over your dirty laundry...)

All these types of causes contain a rationale that absolves you of responsibility.

Category 2: The Child

When the main rationale serves to either avoid discomfort or justify defiance.

"I really want to lose weight, but I just love sweets..."
"I want to stay on budget, but I just can't say no to this shirt..."
"I really want to find a serious relationship, but I just can't see settling down..."
"I know sex is important for my marriage, but I'm just too tired..."

All those could also read "...but I just don't want to." As a child, all that really matters is what you want or don't want, because your parents are responsible for insuring that your actual needs are being met. This is a mindset that we can often carry into adulthood if we aren't careful.

Category 3: The Flower

This is when the primary objective is to protect yourself against an imminent doom.

"What if I fail?"
"What if they don't like it?"
"What if I'm not good enough?"
"What if I get hurt?"

All of these causes contain a rationale that caters to the fear of a potential risk. This specific identity is unique because it usually precedes any action at all, where the others tend to impede what has already begun.

When you make these excuses, it's as if you temporarily assume each of their identities, along with their associated rationale.

Now, I need you to recall back a few pages to a point I made in Self Honesty. I explained how our subconscious beliefs create our conscious thoughts. This point comes directly into play here, when addressing the toxicity of excuses.

Our subconscious mind does not have thoughts; it has beliefs. It is the genesis of our enter belief system about everything: ourselves, the world, others, etc. From these beliefs, our thoughts are produced. ***Our conscious mind has thoughts that are formed from core beliefs***. Beliefs can exist without thoughts because they give birth to thoughts, but thoughts cannot exist without beliefs. Our thoughts simply represent our beliefs. Thoughts then give birth to feelings. Typically our feelings act as the decisive factor in our decision making, which is really risky business if our thoughts are based on distorted core beliefs. So, to recap...

Beliefs > Thoughts > Feelings

(Are we tracking here? It can get a little confusing, I know. Don't hesitate to go back and re-read.)

Understanding this, I want you to look back over the excuses made by each identity. They are statements resulting from thoughts, meaning they must represent the belief system to which they are connected. By making the excuse, you are not only accepting the conscious rationale, but you are adopting the negative belief system from which it is produced as well. Now I want you to switch your brain to begin identifying the self belief systems at work behind the rationale of each identity. If you listen closely enough, their voices speak a horrifying story– one that paints a pretty awful picture of who they think they are.

Let's listen in...

The Victim believes:
"I'm powerless."
"I have no control over my life."
"I am useless."
"I can't affect my future."
"Everything I do is pointless."
"I don't matter."
"I'm not responsible."

The Child believes:
"Someone else needs to take care of me, because

I'm not capable."
"I'm not responsible for my life, someone else is."
"What I want is all that matters."
"I'm not competent enough to be an adult."
"I'm dependent."

The Flower believes:
   "I am weak."
   "I am breakable."
   "I am frail."
   "I am not strong enough to endure pain."
   "I am not good enough."

Read back over those again.

Those are the potential self beliefs you are **affirming** when you give into excuses– directly accepting them as true! I have the feeling that if someone else said those things about you, you wouldn't accept them. So why then, are you willing to accept them when they come from within? These lies are actually a poison– one that becomes the perfect hindrance intended to prevent you from: becoming who you were meant to be, fulfilling your God-given purpose, and meeting the needs of those around you that desperately need what only you can offer. All this is the result of you being stopped dead in your tracks by a lie.

Do you see the tragedy?

Excuses act as masks, disguising your fears in order to present them to you in a way that seems beneficial when they are not. By choosing to remove excuses from your life, you are actually choosing to face your fears and overcome them! This isn't an easy thing to do— I know. It's often so scary that some people simply never do it. It proves too difficult to face the fact that they actually *do* believe they are weak, scared, or inadequate. They allow their fears to grow so large that most of their time ends up being devoted to simply avoiding them. They hide themselves behind a shield of excuses, believing they're protected. Yet, that is the exact lie. The shield they are trusting for their very protection is the exact thing that's harming them! The fears they are desperately trying to avoid are the exact beliefs they end up affirming.

And they wonder why they are disappointed, unhappy, discontent, or depressed.

When you become a person determined to carry out your purpose, excuses are not taken lightly. They are seen as an assault against your character, designed to steal from you the fulfillment and joy of life. It becomes your top priority to protect yourself against them by exposing what they really are: lies.

Lies and fears.

Then you choose to invalidate them by declaring what you DO believe about who you KNOW you are!

Instead of the Victim, you become a fighter, tasked to protect all that affects your purpose because you bear a responsibility to do so. You protect your character because it is your most cherished investment. You fight against the lie that obstacles must stop you from achieving what you were born to do. Instead, you believe they are simply challenges to be overcome. You forge your own solutions even if they're not exactly the way you wanted, because you know your reward is great and nothing will take that from you. You push through no matter what because your eye is on the goal. You are jealous of your joy and will eliminate any threat posed against it.

Instead of the Child, you become an adult, taking responsibility for your life. You understand that no one is coming to save you other than yourself and you step up to that challenge. You recognize it's time to grow up and do what is best for you, even when you don't want to. You embrace the process of maturity and decide to bear your own burdens.

Instead of the Flower, you become a soldier, confidently owning the strength of your character. You look back at all you have overcome, all you have survived and realize you are anything but weak. You understand that enduring failure and disappointment has sharpened your resolve and given you wisdom. You know you are not fragile; you are not breakable. You are capable and willing to do whatever God has asked of you because you know that He empowers you to do so. You decide that no challenge is big enough to break the spirit within you. You have trust in the Creator of the universe that He would not assign you a task that you are incapable of completing. You walk with your head high knowing you are a reflection of His beautiful and perfect image.

That is how you unleash the warrior that is inside of you.

3. Personal Integrity

You could have all the knowledge, resources, and abilities you need to create an amazing life, yet render it all completely useless if you lack one specific thing:

Discipline.

To the purposed person, that kind of waste is simply intolerable. When you have a deep understanding of the value you possess, and the necessity of your purpose to the world, the development of self discipline is no longer an option. It's mandatory. The only variable is the efficiency with which it's developed. Thats why the third and last skill I present to you is the concept of Personal Integrity. I believe it is crucial to the process of developing sustainable self discipline as part of your character, not just your mood.

Let's explore this skill from an angle you may have never thought about before...

The most common approach I see people take when attempting to develop self discipline is what I consider to be "behavior" heavy. This is an approach where you focus primarily on learning skills that aim to help you manage your daily actions. You focus on things that are designed to improve your decision making and help you exercise self control. If I took this approach, I would fill the remaining pages of this chapter with tips and tricks that would help you: finally get up on time, or finally put down the donut, or finally stick to that budget! It would fill your brain with compelling content that would stimulate an emotional desire to *"really get it right this time."* Maybe you'd even stick to it for a week or two!

But guess what?

Once your will power runs out, you'll go right back to your old habits. Why? Because that approach only targets the behavioral aspect of self discipline, leaving out the equally central aspect of emotional awareness (a.k.a the motivation).

Within the very definition of Self Discipline we see two things: "The ability to control one's feelings and overcome one's weaknesses; the ability to pursue what one thinks is right despite temptation to abandon it." The first 6 words reveal that self discipline is the result of two different psychological processes occurring simultaneously: cognitive and emotional. Cognition is the process involved in decision making, acquisition and understanding of knowledge, and the formation of beliefs and attitudes. Emotional (or volitional) processing is involved in wanting and intending, and drive or motivation. The ability to *control* one's feelings requires that we exhibit cognitive control over our feelings which requires emotional awareness. (You can't control something you aren't aware of.)

This is why a "behavior" heavy approach can leave a person frustrated, just as a "feeling" heavy approach will leave someone underestimating the importance of choice. A dual focus is the key. It can diffuse much of the difficulty we face in developing self discipline because it provides balance. Without this approach, it can feel as though we're spinning our wheels, getting nowhere. Since there are so many areas in our lives that require discipline, without it we can begin to resemble a game of whack-a-mole. Thing after thing will keep popping up, one after the other, taking your energy and wasting it. This eventually leaves you 'checked out' thinking *"screw it all, I give up."* So instead of constantly trying to manage your behaviors, or waiting until you *feel* like "being disciplined" I want you to begin to lock your focus on *why you are determined to be a person of integrity!* This will result in the management of your actions.

What is Personal Integrity?

Personal integrity is when your actions **toward yourself** align with what you believe **about yourself**. In other words, the way you treat yourself matches how you feel about yourself. To develop this requires examining your self-beliefs in order to know what they are. If you aren't aware of them you can't possibly act in congruence with them. This is what the first two skills help you do. So then, you take conscious steps to behave in ways that are consistent with them. When applied to self discipline, personal integrity teaches you to value the commitments you make to yourself as highly as those you make to others, because they are seen as an expression of self respect.

I'll give you an example..

If I asked you to meet me at the gym everyday at 4:00 PM for one week, I bet you'd show up and be on time. But, if I asked you to go to the gym by yourself everyday at 4:00 PM for a week, I'd bet your arrival times would vary and you'd probably miss a few days.

Why?

This is because you tend to value your commitments to other people more highly than the ones you make to yourself. It's as if you value other people's time (or the like) higher than your own– which should not be the case. Personal integrity teaches you to begin seeing the way you treat yourself as a reflection of your self esteem, making your personal commitments valuable and worth keeping. If you commit to it, you stick to it– no matter what. It is from this motivation that you should desire to discipline your own actions. (If you struggle with low self esteem, don't think that this doesn't apply to you. That is **not** the case. This skill can actually help you to build your self respect! The more you act like you respect yourself, the more you actually will. It's pretty cool!)

The Role of Choice

Generally, if you have a choice to make, it means you've been presented with multiple different options for results, leaving you to choose the option that best delivers the result you want. Whichever one you choose is selected based on a source of reasoning or motivation. It's really a simple process: the strongest motivation wins. Do you see why the personal integrity as a motivator is so important? This realization is what I want you to begin using to your advantage. By developing your desire to exhibit personal integrity, you are strengthening it to become the most influential factor at decision time. If emotional impulse tries to take over, compelling you to abandon your goal in lieu of immediate pleasure, you aren't left defenseless. You have a weapon to combat that, ensuring you stay on course– as opposed to relying strictly on will power, which can become weak and exhausted.

At the end of the day, discipline comes down to a choice. No matter how strong your internal motivation is, you can still choose against it because you have free will. Your choices direct your life. There are no shortcuts around that, regardless of how desperately we search for them. The truth is, if you want to move forward in life, you have to choose right over wrong, healthy over unhealthy, and smart over easy, in the precise moments that you don't want to. *The belief that there is an "easier route" is a lie, leading people to a life of waiting and irresponsibility.* The people you know who are self disciplined are no different than you are; they simply make certain choices through out the day that align with their personal integrity.

Way too often, we set grandiose goals that are unrealistic and illogical, and then judge ourselves when we fail. We become discouraged and disappointed by our inability to follow through. This defeat usually detours us from future attempts because we think it's a waste of time, inadvertently absolving ourselves of responsibility to do what we wanted to do in the first place!

That is so silly. (Not to mention self manipulative....)

Think about it. Let's say you struggle to get through one day without eating too much sugar, so you decide to do a 30 day cleanse. By setting the mental and physical marker of success at 30 days, you've just set yourself up for failure. Why would you expect yourself to survive 30 days when you struggle with one– merely because you said you would? Typically this approach is unsuccessful and ineffective. It is harmful to your self trust. What I suggest as the solution is very simple: make smaller goals. Every goal you have should be broken up into daily, weekly, bi-weekly and monthly "markers." Each marker being a new opportunity to build (or restore) self trust, moving you along to the next. So, determine to accomplish that 30 day cleanse by way of 4 weekly cleanses, with a mid week accountability check in after you've completed your daily food log... (I hope you're seeing my point here.) Build your self trust day by day, or hour by hour if needed.

The act of setting a goal does not indicate you are able to meet it. The decisive factor lies in your level of forethought and personal integrity. Your choices direct your life, but that doesn't mean you can't do things to help yourself make the best ones.

In conclusion, approaching self discipline from the perspective of personal integrity inspires you to value your personal commitments because they are a reflection of your self respect. It empowers you to manage your daily choice with precision, resulting in intentional and careful living. Self discipline is not only the single most important tool in your possession to achieve your goals, but it is a direct contributor to your self esteem and confidence. By believing you are worth the effort required to stick to that eating plan, or to stay on that budget, you are enlisting a motivation that lasts much longer than the present moment. Whatever it is you determine to do, do it knowing your character is on the line, not just that immediate choice. Any way in which you choose to compromise that, know that you may be jeopardizing the fulfillment of your purpose.

Action Steps

- Take the time to write down 5 things that have been holding you back from accomplishing a goal and apply the excuse filter to them.

- Set aside 10 minutes per day, for 1 week to meditate and listen to your thoughts. Decide to write down atlas 10 that stick out to you.

- Find an accountability partner to begin exercising personal integrity with. Make a goal, share it with each other, and track the progress you both make.

Chapter 4
Balance

*"Every man must decide whether he will walk
in the light of creative altruism or in the
darkness of destructive selfishness."*
– Martin Luther King Jr.

T o be perfectly honest, out of all the points made in this book, this chapter is the hardest for me to write. Not because the thoughts escape me but because the message is so dear to my heart that to express it is an act of vulnerability. So you may feel a different energy or notice a more personal style of writing because I'm going to speak to you very candidly; as if we were sitting across from each other, chatting over a steaming cup of coffee.

So here goes...

If you want to experience joy, go help someone else.
If you want to change your life, think compassionately.
If you want to be happy, give more than you ever receive.

Those three statements hold as much wisdom as the last three chapters. Yet sometimes when something is to simple we don't accept it. We assume that because it's so simple we must be missing something. We write it off as ridiculous, thinking "that can't possibly be all there is to it."

But it is.

I wouldn't be able to sleep at night if I knew you reached the end of this book without hearing the most important message of all, which I have left for last. I am speaking from my soul to yours and I need you to get this.

If you struggle with any level of depression, anxiety, sadness, or pain– I have been there. I know what emptiness feels like, whether its overwhelming or subtle. I know how chilling loneliness can be. I know how sadness can take minutes and turn them into hours, taunting you like a recurring nightmare. I know what it feels like to think you don't matter. I know how weird it is to be suffocating on your own anxiety and confusion and anger, while everyone else's life seems to continue on normally. I know the fear that comes from not knowing the right decision to make, yet having to make one anyway.

If I had never been there I would have no business speaking about how to deal with it.

But I have.

There are two things I can tell you:

1. Pain (regardless of severity) is a tricky thing. It becomes all consuming, requiring most of your energy and focus. All you want to do is escape it. You want it to be over. You wish your life was fun, you wish you felt better, you wish you were 'normal,' etc. Yet all of those thoughts are self focused. That is what pain does. It makes you think about YOU.

Now, I have to tread carefully here because there are different circumstances in life that bring different types of pain. I understand this fully and it does not change my point. To an extent, I cannot speak to the one living with a terminal illness because I have never experienced that; nor to the one who has lost a spouse or a child because I have never experienced that. However, I submit to you that the cause is not whats relevant here. Regardless of the source, the effect of that pain is typically the same. It shifts your focus back to yourself. Whether you think that's right or wrong or good or bad is your choice, all I am submitting to you is that it's true.

The problem is that sometimes the more you focus on fixing your pain, the worse it gets. I believe this is because it is based on an inward focus. Although I am a strong advocate of healthy introspection, there is a delicate line between doing it effectively and doing it ineffectively. How to achieve this balance is made possible by altruistic living.

You must immerse yourself in compassion.

Everything about Selfless Development is based on the 'awareness of others.' You are aware of how your purpose is something that others need you to fulfill; you are aware that your meaning in life bears effect on others; you are aware that God has given you a specific task that He would like you to fulfill; you are aware that your life is integral to the design of the universe. All of those mindsets take your focus and point it outward. You don't wake up and decide to make good choices that day because you want to 'be happy.' You make good choices because you need to take care of the vessel that's responsible for carrying out a very precious mission. (That vessel is you.) That is the basis of the mindset shift that occurs when developing yourself self-lessly.

As you begin to teach your mind to focus on others, you will activate the instinct to help those around you.

It becomes almost impulsive. It's no longer seen as a choice, rather a duty.

Now, for the sake of clarity, let me tell you what I don't consider to be altruistic living: the occasional volunteer event every year around the holidays; the sympathetic face of sadness after tiptoeing around the homeless guy sleeping on the sidewalk; handing out a Nutrigrain bar to the beggar at the stop light after realizing its been in your car for a week.

Are any of those things wrong? Nope. But they aren't what I'm talking about.

Living an altruistic lifestyle is so rare that those who actually do it are elevated to something close to Sainthood. That alone implies it is a rarity. This disturbs me greatly.

Why are more people not aware of the duty to care and love those who are less fortunate than them? No one really focuses on that. They are usually too busy wondering why they are unhappy and 'stuck' in life.

Coincidental, huh?

On one hand, I understand that you could feel like the time to give is when you have something to give.

However, that logic fails to realize that the exact time to give is when you have NOTHING to give. Our souls do not operate the same way our physical bodies do. When we are tired, we cannot go run a marathon. Our muscles will give out, our lungs will collapse, etc. However, when our souls are experiencing fatigue from pain, it is by giving love that we are reenergized. It is by caring for others that we are distracted from our own issues. We were designed to GIVE our way to healing; GIVE our way to peace; GIVE our way to restoration.

If you want joy, it's simple. Give.

Conclusion

I began this book by explaining the role that gratitude plays in our lives. Specifically, how it creates within us the ability to properly value our purpose—enough to discover it and fulfill it. I explained that gratitude should be our entire root system, setting a firm foundation for the rest of our lives to blossom from. Without it, our entire structure can cave in on itself– leaving us sad, empty, and lost.

I said in the very beginning of the preface that the reason I wrote this book is because I want you to understand joy, yet I've spent very little time actually talking about it and a lot of time talking about gratitude and purpose.

Coincidental? Nope.

I suggest that they are actually synonymous. *Without gratitude we can't experience joy and without purpose we can't find fulfillment.* The most fascinating part about gratitude is that it not only supports our structure, it sustains it and completes it.

When you choose to view life through The Purpose Perspective and apply The Freedom Formula into your daily life, it becomes as if a floor made of glass has been installed in your soul. Beneath it, flows a gulf of joy and peace. Above it, exists your normal everyday life. No matter if it's your best day or your worst day, nothing is able to break through that glass floor and disturb your balance. Nothing can break you past a certain point. Its as if you have entered into an alternate reality in which you understand the concept of peace that surpasses all understanding.

You become a different kind of person– one that is whole in every way. You are a cup that is not just half full or half empty, but filled to overflowing. You know who you are, who's you are, what you are and for what you are meant to live. Life is not perfect for you, but you have accepted that your meaning is too valuable to jeopardize. You've spent time developing the internal skills needed to overcome life's challenges and remove all excuses. **Your lifestyle is aligned with your priorities.** You are unstoppable because you have accessed a force that reaches beyond your own comfort zone. You are a person on a mission and whatever it is that attempts to detour you from accomplishing it better be really serious before you pay it any mind. You care for your soul because your primary concern is developing its quality. You walk with a spirit of confidence knowing that the Creator of the universe has found you worthy of a special purpose. That revelation is nothing short of humbling– creating a unique blend of confident humility. You are in awe that you get to experience grace on a daily basis merely by existing. The days you wake up exhausted or weak or confused, you fall back on the truth of Gods purpose on your life to anchor you back to reality.

All of this is the result of following God's divinely designed structure for how you should operate internally. He equipped you with everything you need in order to do what He asks of you but He mandates that you first, must appreciate His deity. You must acknowledge and thank Him for His love.

You must be grateful.

This gratefulness cannot only exist within your self as thoughts and feelings. That is just not enough. It has to be put into action.

Acknowledgements

You're probably aware that writing a book is hard. Like really hard. Like so hard you want to want to light your own hair on fire just because. You become that annoying person who's obsessed with their book, while everyone around you politely listens as you yammer on about it for months.

So, here's to those who listened while I yammered.

Josiah, you are the reason this book isn't about an octopus.

Dad, thanks for fighting. I need you around for many more years.

God, you're seriously my homie.

Oh, and wine.
I love you, wine.